HUNTLY
CASTLE

Chris Tabraham

EDITED BY CHRIS TABRAHAM
ILLUSTRATED BY MICHELLE MCCLUSKIE,
DAVID SIMON AND DAVE POLLOCK
PHOTOGRAPHY BY HISTORIC SCOTLAND PHOTOGRAPHIC UNIT
PRODUCED BY ROY STEWART PRINT SERVICES
PRINTED IN SCOTLAND FROM SUSTAINABLE MATERIALS
BY BUCCLEUCH PRINTERS LTD., HAWICK

FIRST PUBLISHED BY HMSO 1985
THIS REVISED EDITION FIRST PUBLISHED BY HISTORIC SCOTLAND 1995
REPRINTED 2004
CROWN COPYRIGHT © HISTORIC SCOTLAND 1995
ISBN 1 903570 27 1

INTRODUCTION

"For he [the marquis] *was so much taken up with his newe buildings, standing by his masons, urging their diligencies, and directing and judging their worke, that he had scarce tyme to eate, or sleep, much less to wreat."*

(REVEREND GILBERT BLAKHALL,

A VISITOR TO THE CASTLE IN 1643)

Huntly Castle, the ancient seat of the Gordons, is a noble ruin in a beautiful setting. It is remarkable both for the splendour of its architecture and for its stirring history.

The castle served as a baronial residence for five centuries and underwent several transformations before reaching its present form. The surviving remains give us the story of the development of the Scottish castle, from the motte and bailey of the twelfth century, through the tower-house castle of the later middle ages, to the stately stone palace of the seventeenth century.

The castle is memorable also as the scene of events famous in Scotland's history. The early stronghold gave shelter to Robert the Bruce during his struggle with England in the early fourteenth century, and the first stone castle witnessed the climax of the struggle between the Stewart king, James II, and the over-powerful Black Douglas family. The place was the resort of kings and queens, coming sometimes with friendly, sometimes with hostile, purpose. At the time of the Reformation in the 1560s it suffered outrage upon outrage. During the Civil War of the following century it was held in the monarch's name, for which its lord died on the scaffold. In the last efforts of the Stewarts to regain the throne of Great Britain the castle was garrisoned against them.

An impression of how Huntly Castle may have looked during Rev. Gilbert Blakhall's visit in 1643.

THE STORY OF HUNTLY CASTLE

THE PEEL OF STRATHBOGIE

*T*he twelfth century was one of momentous change for Scotland as her kings, David I, Malcolm IV and William I set about recasting the whole social and political structure of the country. By William's death in 1214 the old Celtic kingdom had been transformed into a feudal country. But that change was not achieved without resistance, particularly from the strongly Celtic areas of the north and west.

The province of Moray in the north-east put up a spirited resistance for more than a century and a half before being brought to account by Alexander II in 1230. Its subjugation was achieved largely through the placing of loyal subjects at strategic points along the main routes leading thereto. One of the most important routes led northwards by Kildrummy through Strathbogie to Rothes, Elgin and Inverness. The crossing of the River Deveron at its confluence with the River Bogie was critical and here, by the late twelfth century, King William had settled Duncan (II), earl of Fife. Choosing the defensible position between the Bogie and the Deveron, Earl Duncan built the first castle, known as the 'Peel of Strathbogie'.

THE CASTLE AND ROBERT THE BRUCE

The lands of Strathbogie passed to David, third son of the earl of Fife, before the end of that century. His grandson, also David, became earl of Atholl through marriage in about 1264 but died on crusade at Tunis six years later. John of Strathbogie, who succeeded him, was a loyal follower of Robert the Bruce and died fighting his cause in 1306, the first earl to be executed in England for over 200 years.

In the following year, during his campaign against the Comyns, King Robert himself was brought to the castle at Strathbogie after falling ill at Inverurie. He recovered and went on to crush the Comyn family but, although Bruce had found shelter in the castle, David of Strathbogie, the new lord, was foolish enough to turn against his sovereign shortly before the king's great triumph at Bannockburn in 1314. As punishment, David forfeited his lands, which King Robert then granted to Sir Adam Gordon of Huntly, in Berwickshire - from which place the old castle of Strathbogie was ultimately to receive its new name.

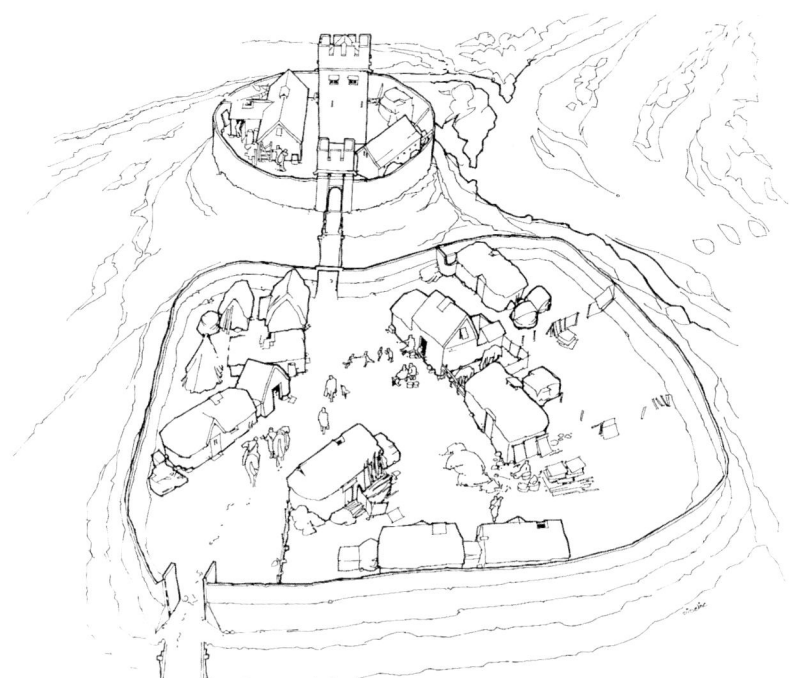

An impression of how the Peel of Strathbogie may have looked about 1200.

THE GORDONS OF HUNTLY

It was not until 1376 that the Gordons settled down in unchallenged occupation of their new lordship, as the earls of Atholl retained certain claims until their extinction at this date. In 1408 Sir John Gordon, last in the male line of the Gordons of Huntly and Strathbogie, was succeeded by his sister Elizabeth, who in that year married Sir Alexander Seton. Either of these two gentlemen could have been responsible for the erection of the new stone tower house, on the north side of the bailey, to replace the out-dated timber castle built over 200 years before.

The boar's head, an heraldic device of the Gordons, carved on the south front of the castle.

In 1436 Sir Alexander was created first Lord Gordon, and either in 1445 or 1449 his son, also Alexander, was made first earl of Huntly. His descendants have held the castle ever since.

THE CASTLE AND THE BLACK DOUGLASES

In 1452 the bitter struggle between the Crown and the Black Douglas family reached its climax. The earl of Huntly stood for the King and hurried south to aid his sovereign but was hastily recalled after receiving unwelcome news. In his absence the earl of Moray, a kinsman of Douglas, had descended on Strathbogie, wasted the lands and burnt the castle. Arriving quickly on the scene, Huntly cleared the invaders from the strath, pursued them across the Spey and broke the power of the Morayshire Douglases.

The annihilation of the Black Douglases that followed shortly after increased the power and standing of the earl of Huntly and the growing dignity of the family was probably reflected in a major refashioning of their castle at Strathbogie. The new building, on the south side of the bailey (now represented by the basement storey only), was still unfinished when the first earl died there in 1470 and the work was completed by his son, George, the second earl.

The monumental tomb of Alexander Gordon, first earl of Huntly (died 1470), in St Mary's Aisle, Elgin Cathedral. The effigy, badly defaced most probably during the Reformation in 1560, shows the earl in the robe of lord chancellor of Scotland with a dagger hanging from his girdle.

THE CASTLE OF HUNTLY

The grandeur of the new castle and the importance of the Gordons secured it numerous visits from royalty and others of distinction. In January 1496 the marriage of Perkin Warbeck, pretender to the English throne, to Lady Catherine Gordon, the 'White Rose of Scotland', was celebrated with much pomp at the castle in James IV's presence. James was a frequent visitor and the royal accounts detail the expenses which he incurred in gaming, in paying his minstrels and in gifts to a Moorish juggler. Two payments of 'drinksilver' to masons, in 1501 and 1505, show that building work was going on at the castle.

In 1506 Alexander, the third earl, received a charter confirming him in his lands providing that his *"chief messuage, which was formerly called Strathbogie, be in all future times named the Castle of Huntly"*.

THE CASTLE AND THE TWO QUEEN MARYS

George, the fourth earl, became lord chancellor of Scotland in 1547 and in 1550 travelled to France with Mary of Guise, widow of James V. His lofty station and new-found wealth, coupled with what he must have seen on his visit to the Continent, prompted him to remodel his castle comprehensively. His *"new expensive stately building, which he had joined to the old castle and rendered a very convenient palace"* was ready in time for the visit in 1556 of Mary of Guise, now the queen-regent. The reception Mary received was magnificent. She was met by a guard of honour of 1000 men, and the splendour of her entertainment was such that, after a few days, she wished to depart so as to relieve the burden on her host. Huntly assured her that his cheer was within his means and astonished her by displaying the spacious vaults crammed with provisions. Queen Mary was doubtless impressed but her adviser, the French ambassador, recommended that she find an early opportunity to 'clip his wings'. In the event it was her daughter, Mary Queen of Scots, who did just that.

The earl of Huntly held fast to Catholicism and his castle became in effect the Scottish headquarters of the Roman Church during the Reformation. Mary Queen of Scots, who began her personal reign in 1561, was at heart a supporter of the old religion

The badly-weathered coat-of-arms of George, fourth earl of Huntly, impaled with those of his lady,
Elizabeth Keith, high up on the north front of the palace.

but political considerations and the independent bearing of Huntly persuaded the young queen to move against him. In August 1562 she left Holyrood Palace for the north-east and on 28 October the two met in battle at Corrichie, on the Hill o' Fare, 12 miles (20 km) west of Aberdeen. Huntly himself fell off his horse and died, but his two sons were taken. The elder boy was spared but the younger one, Sir John, was beheaded before the queen at Aberdeen. Their castle was wrecked and the contents looted. The inventory taken presents a most impressive picture of the wealth and splendour of its lord; this included all the treasures of Aberdeen Cathedral, including the silk tent in which Edward II has slept the night before Bannockburn, a gift to the cathedral from Robert the Bruce.

THE MARQUISATE OF HUNTLY

The extent of the damage wrought in 1562 is not known. Work on the fabric was still proceeding in July 1594 when the English ambassador reported that *"Huntly hastens the building of his hall and gallery at Strathbogy"*. But in October of that year the castle sustained a second and far more serious blow. Having become suspect through his alleged connections with the mysterious plot of the 'Spanish Blanks', George, the sixth earl, joined Lord Erroll in a mad revolt. After some success the rebels were put to flight and James VI was soon before Huntly Castle with gunpowder given to him by the townsfolk of Aberdeen. The 'greate olde tower' on the north side of the bailey was blown up but damage to the main palace appears to have been minimal.

Medallion portraits of George Gordon, first marquis, and Henrietta Stewart, first marchioness, together with their arms and mottoes, sculpted on a fireplace in the palace.

In 1597 the earl made his peace with King James and two years later was created the first marquis of Huntly. He immediately set about repairing and embellishing his damaged residence. By March 1606 (the date on one of the fireplaces) the work must have been well-nigh complete and the stately row of oriel windows with their inscription, the grand doorway with its stunning armorial frontispiece, and the exquisitely-carved fireplaces surely presented one of the most splendid architectural sights of the day. The enforced exile of the sixth earl in France following the debacle in 1594 may have inspired this ambitious and sophisticated remodelling.

George, second marquis of Huntly. (Courtesy of the National Galleries of Scotland.)

THE FINAL YEARS

The building works put in hand by the first marquis were not the last, for George, the second marquis, *"was so much taken up"*, noted a visiting priest in 1643, *"with his new buildings, from four hours in the morning until eight at night, standing by his masons, urging their diligencies, and directing and judging their work, that he had scarce tyme to eate, or sleep, much less to wreat* (write)*"*. His master-mason, George Thomson, had previously rebuilt the 'imperial crown' of King's College tower, Aberdeen, after it was blown down in 1633.

Thereafter the story is one of ruin and decay. The second marquis stood for his king in the Civil War and sealed his devotion on the scaffold. *"You may take my head from my shoulders"*, he told the Covenanters, *"but not my heart from my sovereign"*. His castle suffered sorely for the loyalty of its lord. In 1640 it was occupied by the Covenanters' army and the parson of Rothiemay tells how the house *"was preserved from being rifled or defaced, except some emblems and imagerye, which looked somewhat popish and superstitious lycke; and therefor, by the industry of one captain James Wallace, wer hewd and brocke doune off the frontispiece of the house; but all the rest of the frontispeece containing Huntly's scutcheon, etc, was left untwoched, as it standes to this daye"*. The truth of that statement is evident on the frontispiece today.

In 1644 the castle was briefly held by the duke of Montrose, and in 1647 it was gallantly defended against General Leslie by Lord Charles Gordon, but its garrison was starved into surrender. Savage treatment was meted out; the men were hanged and their officers beheaded. In 1650 Charles II visited briefly on his way to his coronation at Scone. The castle last saw action during the '45 Jacobite Rising, when it was occupied by Government troops. Thereafter it became a stone quarry until antiquarian sentiment in the nineteenth century came to the rescue of the noble pile. In 1923 the duke of Richmond and Gordon entrusted the ruin into State care and in 1925 Sir Leybourne Davidson of Huntly Lodge presented to the nation the fine tree-lined avenue by which the castle is approached.

John Claud Nattes' sketch of the south front, made in 1799 when much of the palace was still roofed and a truly impressive spectacle.

A SHORT TOUR

1. MOTTE
AN ARTIFICIAL MOUND CREATED IN THE LATE 12TH CENTURY ON WHICH STOOD THE WOODEN RESIDENCE OF EARL DUNCAN (II) OF FIFE.

2. BAILEY
AN ARTIFICIAL PLATFORM CREATED AT THE SAME TIME AS THE MOTTE [1] AS A SERVICE AREA FOR THE CASTLE, AND WHERE THE LATER STONE CASTLE BUILDINGS WERE CONCENTRATED.

3. TOWERHOUSE
BUILT AFTER THE GORDONS ACQUIRED THE LORDSHIP IN 1376 TO REPLACE THE WOODEN TOWER ON THE MOTTE [1] AS THE LORD'S PRIVATE RESIDENCE. AN L-PLAN BUILDING NOW REPRESENTED BY LOW STONE WALLS BUT ONCE LOFTY AND IMPRESSIVE. IT WAS BLOWN UP BY JAMES VI IN 1594.

4. PALACE
BEGUN IN THE MID 15TH CENTURY BY THE 1ST EARL AS AN ADJUNCT TO HIS TOWER HOUSE [3], COMPREHENSIVELY REMODELLED IN THE MID 16TH CENTURY BY THE 4TH EARL TO REPLACE THE TOWER HOUSE AS THE MAIN RESIDENCE, AND GREATLY EMBELLISHED ABOUT 1600 BY THE 1ST MARQUIS.

5. WEST RANGE
A 16TH-CENTURY TWO-STOREY RANGE WITH ATTIC NOW REPRESENTED BY LOW STONE WALLS BUT ONCE HOUSING EXTRA DOMESTIC ACCOMMODATION ABOVE A SERVICE BASEMENT.

HUNTLY CASTLE

6. BAKEHOUSE AND BREWHOUSE
A 16TH-CENTURY SERVICE BLOCK
PROVIDING THE CASTLE HOUSEHOLD
WITH ITS STAPLE DIET OF BAKING AND
ALE.

7. STABLE
OF UNCERTAIN DATE, BUT POSSIBLY
EARLY 17TH-CENTURY, WITH PROVISION
FOR TEN STALLS.

8. EAST RANGE
PART OF THE BUILDING WORKS CARRIED
OUT FOR THE 2ND MARQUIS IN THE
EARLY 17TH CENTURY. IT INCLUDED A
ONCE-FINE ENTRANCE GATE.

9. OUTBUILDINGS
OF UNCERTAIN DATE AND FUNCTION,
BUT POSSIBLY SERVICE
ACCOMMODATION LINKED TO THE
15TH-CENTURY TOWER HOUSE [3].

10. RAVELIN
AN EARTHEN MOUND FORMED DURING
THE CIVIL WAR IN THE 1640S TO
PROVIDE A SHELTERED ARTILLERY
DEFENCE.

11. ROADWAY
A COBBLED TRACK ONCE GIVING ACCESS
TO THE CASTLE BUT ABANDONED BY
THE EARLY 17TH CENTURY.

Artist's bird's-eye view of the castle from the east.

THE ARCHITECTURE OF HUNTLY CASTLE

THE MOTTE AND BAILEY

The stately ruins of the later medieval stone castle stand upon the remnant of its predecessor, a motte and bailey castle built in the later twelfth century by Earl Duncan (II) of Fife. This first castle was constructed largely of timber and was placed upon two artificial mounds of uneven size; the smaller but higher **motte** supported the earl's house, while the more extensive but lower **bailey** contained ancillary buildings, such as the hall, chapel, stables and other residential and service accommodation (see the reconstruction drawing on page 5). A wide, deep **ditch** separated the motte from its bailey, both of which probably had wooden palisades round their summits, and steeply sloping sides.

The motte has not subsequently been built over and appears now as a grass-covered, flat-topped conical mound over 24 m in diameter. The bailey to its east was the focus of the later castle and is now largely covered by buildings. The motte and bailey remained in use for some two centuries. Only when the Gordons of Huntly came into possession in the later fourteenth century was there a radical revision of the accommodation.

The three castles at Huntly. In the background is the motte, or castle mound, built in the late twelfth century. The bailey, or outer court, of this first castle (in the foreground) has subsequently housed the later castles - the stone tower house (right foreground), built about 1400, and the palace (on the left) begun about 1460, greatly remodelled in the 1550s, and further embellished about 1600.

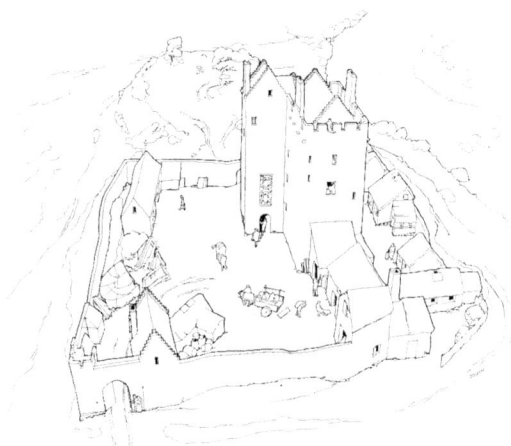

An impression of how the tower-house castle might have looked in the fifteenth century.

THE TOWER HOUSE

Quite when the first stone castle was built is not known but the form it took - a thick-walled and lofty L-shaped **tower house** (it is called *"the greate olde tower"* in 1594) - may best be ascribed to the late fourteenth or early fifteenth century; in which case it may have been built by either Sir John Gordon (died 1408) or Sir Alexander Seton, his brother-in-law, who succeeded him.

Little more than the foundations of this tower house survive (see the photograph opposite). Indeed, its very existence was not known until excavation works were carried out soon after the castle passed into State care. The meagre remains defy description, but by analogy with tower houses elsewhere we can reasonably assume that the ground floor was used for storage, that the first floor was the hall, the main public room, and that the upper storeys were the lord's private lodging. The winding stair linking all the floors like a vertical corridor would have been within the projecting wing, which gives the tower house its characteristic L-plan. Other than the walls themselves, which are 2.7 m thick, there are no distinguishing features except for the hint that the ground floor in the main block was covered by a stone vault.

The tower house did not stand alone but was surrounded by buildings housing ancillary residential accommodation and other service offices. At least some of the **ruined buildings** to the north of the tower house probably date from this period.

THE PALACE

The castle complex is today dominated by the imposing palace along the south side of the bailey. It has a complicated building history but one which neatly divides into three discrete episodes:

(1) The original building (about 1460) - Probably erected to serve as a great hall, an outer and larger banqueting and reception room to complement the lord's hall in the tower house. Only the basement of this first building survives.

(2) The building remodelled (about 1550) - All but the basement is rebuilt from the ground floor up to provide a new residence, or 'palace', for the lord, to replace the cramped, ill-lit rooms in the tower house.

(3) The building renovated (about 1600) - A major refurbishment of the palace, not so much intended to alter the layout of the accommodation as to greatly embellish it inside and out.

The palace from the south.

The palace from the north-west, with the grassy slope and ditch of the earlier castle mound in the foreground.

THE ORIGINAL BUILDING

(ABOUT 1460)

The overthrow of the Black Douglases in 1455 brought its rewards for the first earl of Huntly, a steadfast supporter of the Crown throughout the bitter struggle. This increased favour, coupled with the fact that Huntly's castle had not escaped unscathed, no doubt prompted the earl into extending and enlarging his residence.

There is much doubt as to what precisely was done at this time for the building was radically altered by the fourth earl a century later. Only the underground **basement** has survived, containing three dark vaulted **storage cellars** in the main block and a grim prison in the projecting round tower. Each cellar has a doorway with a three-sided lintel and a gun-loop of the 'inverted-keyhole' type, both features characteristic of the later fifteenth century.

Plan of the palace at basement level.

The **prison** is reached by a narrow passage, protected by doors at either end; the inner door opens in the stone vault of the prison, over 2 m above its floor. This door has been doubly secured by a wooden door and an iron 'yett' or gate. The prison has been aired by two gun-holes rising through the vault. Otherwise it is featureless.

Of interest, because they reveal most intimately the home-spun life of the household, are the **graffiti** scrawled onto the plastered walls of the basement corridor. They include such diverse subjects as a crusie lamp, a clock dial, pavilion tents, a bull, and men and women in sixteenth-century dress.

One of the cellar doorways.

THE BUILDING REMODELLED

(ABOUT 1550)

George, the fourth earl, became chancellor of Scotland in 1547 and this elevation prompted him to put in train a radical replanning of his castle. His main achievement was the almost complete remodelling of the building which we now call the palace. The earl was probably motivated by the desire to provide a more imposing residence for himself, his family and personal servants, to replace the antiquated lodging in the tower house. The new palace seems to have been completed in time for the visit of Mary of Guise, the queen-regent, in 1556. The date 1553, with the initials of George Gordon, the fourth earl, and those of his wife, Elizabeth Keith, are carved on a skew-stone supporting the crow-stepped west gable of the palace, and midway along the front of the palace, just below the wall-head, a shield displays the arms of the same couple (see the photograph on page 8).

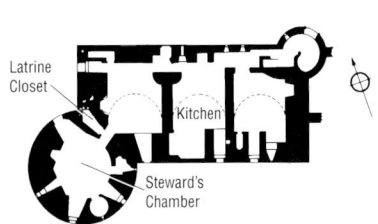

Plan of the palace at ground-floor level.

The steward's chamber in the round tower at ground-floor level.

The **ground floor** comprised a **kitchen** flanked by two **store rooms**. The room in the round tower, directly over the prison, was probably the **steward's chamber**. It is well lit, has a fireplace, a latrine closet, and two stairs giving access to the lord's private chambers on the floor above.

The two store rooms were also converted into private chambers at a later date for their fireplaces are clearly insertions. The kitchen seems to have been retained throughout, its great arched fireplace now sadly dilapidated. There is a waste oulet beneath the hearth and two stone channels in the north wall, the upper one bringing in fresh water and the lower one taking dirty water out to a drain in the courtyard.

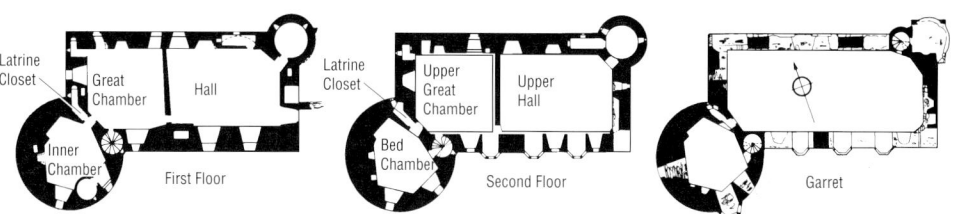

Plans of the three upper floors of the palace.

gunhole

door to
steward's
chamber

remains of
bell-pull
arrangement

The inner chamber of the earl's lodging seen from the bed-recess.

The **first floor** was the earl's lodging. It comprised **three rooms**, two of which are referred to in an interesting tract entitled *The maner of the Erle of Huntlies Death*, describing the apoplectic stroke that carried off the fifth earl in 1576. One was *"the grit chalmer* (great chamber)", also referred to as the *"chalmer of daice* (dais)", and the other *"his owin chalmer...quhilk...was ane round within* (that is, beyond) *the grit chalmer"*. The third room, we may assume, was the earl's hall. This was the conventional arrangement of the day. All three were reception rooms, graded according to the rank of those being received. The **hall**, the largest in size, was the least restricted of the rooms and served also as dining room; the **great chamber** was a more intimate chamber, the ancestor of the drawing room; the **inner chamber** in the round tower was the earl's bedchamber with the bed itself partly recessed into the west wall to the right of the fireplace. Between the great and inner chambers was a **latrine closet**.

The **second floor** was the countess's lodging. It has a similar plan with a sequence of hall, great and inner chambers, and a latrine closet between the latter two rooms.

THE BUILDING RENOVATED

(ABOUT 1600)

The beautiful oriel window high up on the great round tower of the palace.

In 1594 Huntly Castle was badly damaged as a result of the sixth earl's involvement in a mad revolt against his monarch. Banished to France for a short while, he returned home, made his peace with his king and set about repairing his residence. Prompted by his elevation to the marquisate of Huntly in 1597, and doubtless inspired by what he had seen during his exile, he took the opportunity of embellishing his house, inside and out. The result is a spectacular display of heraldic and symbolical enrichment, unique in the British Isles. The work was well-nigh complete by March 1606, the date on one of the fireplaces.

The great heraldic fireplace in the hall of the marchioness's lodging. The coats-of-arms of Huntly and Lennox on the lintel are beautifully rendered, while above them the arms of King James VI and I and his queen, Anne of Denmark, are certainly the finest portrayal surviving in Scotland of the royal arms of the United Kingdom as adjusted after the Union of the Crowns (1603). The mailed figures supporting the lintel seem to have no heraldic significance, but the obelisks on either side of the royal arms, enribboned with the names of the first marquis and marchioness, terminate respectively in the Seton crescent and the Lennox fleur-de-lys. Above the royal arms is a panel from which the sculpture has been chiselled off, and on either side are figures likewise defaced. These were doubtless subjects of a sacred nature which aroused the puritanical anger of Captain James Wallace (see page 11). The sacred verses from Romans 8,28 escaped his wrath:

Sen God doth us defend
ve sal prevail unto the end.
To thaes that love God
Al thingis virkis to the best.

The renovations seem to have been largely cosmetic and not to have greatly altered the fourth earl's arrangement of the accommodation. The most significant changes were the raising of the roof to incorporate the beautiful **suite of oriel windows** and a fine **belvedere** on the south front, the building of a stately **loggia** (a covered open arcade) at ground level further along the south front, where the family could sit in comfort after taking their exercise in the grounds, and the addition of the projecting round stair-tower at the north-east corner with its stunning **frontispiece**.

Internally, both lodgings were greatly enhanced. The fireplaces in the marquis's lodging have been removed by stone robbers long since but traces of the fine **plaster cornices** still adhere to the walls. On the east wall of the great chamber is a spirited sketch of a huntsman and hounds bringing down a deer. The **fireplaces** in the upper lodging, presumably occupied by the marchioness, Henrietta Stewart, have survived and both are marvellous examples of the stone-carver's craft, particularly the great heraldic mantelpiece in the upper hall. The fireplace lintel in the lady's great chamber (see the photograph on page 9) has medallion portraits of the marquis and marchioness.

The fine belvedere (top left) and the splendid suite of oriel windows at the top of the south front with a frieze bearing the inscription (now mutilated at the end):
GEORGE GORDOVN FIRST MARQVIS OF HVNTLIE 16
HENRIETTE STEWART MARQVESSE OF HVNTLIE 02

THE FRONTISPIECE

The greatest triumph of the mason-artist employed by the marquis to enrich his palace is unquestionably the frontispiece over the main doorway. Nothing quite like it exists anywhere else in the country. *"It is probably the most splendid heraldic doorway in the British Isles"*, wrote one Lord Lyon, *"for achievement upon achievement stretches up the side of the tower, connected by delicately moulded panels, so that when all was fresh and emblazoned in colour, and the corbelled turret above was complete, it must have been a truly imposing entrance"*.

The frontispiece has been carefully considered insofar as its arrangement of heraldic and symbolical panels is concerned. As the eye ascends, so it is led successively from lower themes to higher. It begins with the noble marquis and his lady. Above their achievements are those of their sole earthly overlord, the king of Scots and his Danish queen. Above this again the eye is led up to the contemplation of the Divine Power on which all mortal glory depends, of the inheritance in a better world that we are promised by the Passion and the Resurrection of Our Lord. Finally, at the summit of the whole majestic and moving composition, the St Michael group portrays the final triumph of Good over Evil on the day of the Last Judgement.

On the door lintel are four shields bearing, from left to right, - (1) the arms of Huntly; (2) a monogram combining the initials of the first marquis and his lady; (3) the arms of Lennox; (4) the date 1602. Between them are coursing deer-hounds - the Huntly supporters. Over the lintel a long vertical panel has the following subjects, in ascending order:

(1) The impaled arms of the first marquis and his lady (that is, Gordon and Lennox) supported on the dexter (left) side by the collared deer-hound of the Gordons, and on the sinister (right) side by the wolf of Lennox. Both family mottoes - BYDAND and AVAND DARLY (Darnley) - are present; and the coronet carries both the stag's head crest of the Gordons and the bull's head of Lennox.

(2) The royal arms of Scotland (James VI) impaled with those of his queen, Anne of Denmark. The queen's arms include those of Denmark, Norway, Sweden, Gothland and the so-called 'Vandalic Towns' -Danzig, Elbing, Konigsberg, Riga, Stralsund and Wismar. Over all is the Danneborg Cross and a blank inescutcheon, which was presumably painted. The dexter supporter of this splendid shield is the Scottish unicorn carrying the royal banner while the sinister supporter is the Danish wyvern carrying the royal banner of Denmark. Beneath the shield is the badge of St Andrew and, over all, the royal crown with the Scottish lion for crest, and on either side the initials IR6 and ARS for Jacobus Rex Sextus and Anna Regina Scotorum. Above this, on the basal moulding of the next compartment, is the royal motto IN DEFENS.

(3) The Five Wounds of Christ (the pierced Heart, Hands and Feet) with the instruments of His Passion, and two supporting figures, probably St Mary and St John. Above is the text (Galatians 6,14) - ABSIT NOBIS GLORIARI NISI CRUCE DOMINI NOSTRI JESU CHRISTI, *'God forbid that I should glory save in the Cross of our Lord Jesus Christ'*. All these subjects were defaced by Captain Wallace in 1640 (see page 11).

(4) A circular panel (also defaced) displaying the Risen Christ in glory, with a circle of clouds, accompanied by the proclamation DIVINA VIRTUTE RESURGO, *"I rise again with divine power."* On one side of the panel is the Scottish lion and on the other the twin-headed eagle of the Holy Roman Empire. By these emblems we are reminded that the realm of Scotland claimed to be in her own right an imperial power, whose mythical monarch, Achaius - so people fondly imagined - had negotiated a treaty on equal terms with the Emperor Charlemagne. Above all is the figure of St Michael, the warrior archangel, triumphing over Satan. Both the fourth earl and the first marquis were knights of the illustrious French Order of Chivalry.

FURTHER READING

ON THE CASTLE:
W D Simpson 'The Architectural History of Huntly Castle', *Proceedings of the Society of Antiquaries of Scotland*, 56 (1921-2), 134-63
W D Simpson 'Further Notes on Huntly Castle', *Proceedings of the Society of Antiquaries of Scotland*, 67 (1932-3), 137-60

ON SCOTTISH CASTLES GENERALLY:
S Cruden *The Scottish Castle* (1981)
C Tabraham *Scottish Castles and Fortifications* (1990)
C Tabraham *Scotland's Castles* (1997)